Nursery Rhymes for Cats

Julie and John Hope

Contents

CAR CAR BACK SEAT

Sing to: Baa Baa Black Sheep

Car car back seat
I am such a fool
Bribed with biscuits
Veterinary bull

Once for deworming
And once for the shots
Once for a-hurling
And once for the trots

Car car back seat
Waiting with the mutts
Close your eyes and
Hang onto your nuts

❄ ❄ ❄

BLACK CAT AT ME HE SPAT

Sing to: Jack Sprat Could Eat No Fat

Black cat at me he spat
And shouted words obscene
I chased like hell
But tripped and fell
Disgrace was unforeseen

❄ ❄ ❄

SING A SONG OF SIXTH SENSE

Sing to: Sing a Song of Sixpence

Sing a song of sixth sense
You're acting rather sly
I'm never fed at this time
Now look me in the eye

Think I haven't noticed
You packing stuff away?
I won't allow you taking
Another holiday

I won't go to the cattery house
You must think I'm a dummy
To try and fool me yet again
Is really rather crummy

I'll stay here in the garden
You won't find me tonight
For I will find a tall tree
And clamber out of sight

❉ ❉ ❉

ME AND MY BROTHER

Sing to: Old Mother Hubbard

Me and my brother and one or two others
We all were left alone
While Human's away us cats we will play
Wreak havoc and tear up her home

We rummaged in cupboards
And found a nice shawl
It really was joy
To unravel it all

We went to the hamster
To terror and tease
And when we got there
We ate up his cheese

We went to the kitchen
To check out our dish
And up on the counter
We stole us a fish

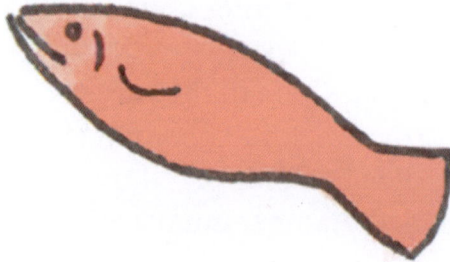

We went to the bathroom
The paper to fetch
It's really amazing
How far it will stretch

We went to the bedroom
To trample the sheets
And next thing we knew
We were all fast asleep

* * *

MARY'S WARY YELLOW CANARIES

Sing to: Mary, Mary Quite Contrary

Mary's wary yellow canaries
Beautiful fat little birds
I dearly wish them in my dish
They're really too scrumptious for words

❋ ❋ ❋

FUSSYCAT FUSSYCAT FUR MUST BE CLEAN

Sing to: Pussycat Pussycat Where Have You Been?

Fussycat fussycat fur must be clean
Look at my dishes and make sure they gleam
Now check all my bedding so there is no hair
And make sure the cushions are laid out with flair

My human is kindly but causes me stress
His house is untidy it's really a mess
So I have a plan which will help him cope
He wil be so grateful, my two-legged dope

I'll shred up these papers in front of the door
And tip out the liquids all over the floor
So when he comes home and he's ready to flop
He's ever so thankful that now he must mop

❄ ❄ ❄

TINKLE TINKLE HOW BIZARRE

Sing to: Twinkle Twinkle Little Star

Tinkle tinkle how bizarre
How do birds know where we are?
Silent stalking through the grass
Leave us standing like an ass

Now when I hunted recently
I always heard a bell near me
And when I jumped to catch my prey
That bird he upped and flew away!

But stranger still and it did foll'r
At the same time I lost my collar
How overnight I cannot guess
My hunting was a great success!

❄ ❄ ❄

MOULDING SOUL

Sing to: Old King Cole

Moulding sole
In my very own bowl
Rubbish from the night before
You call it a treat
Food you wouldn't eat
I definitely will ignore

✳ ✳ ✳

SHE'S BEEN ALL HEART

Sing to: The Queen of Hearts

She's been all heart
A salmon tart
Left cooling on the rack
Now swallow quick
And don't be sick
I hear her coming back!

Now she complained
And I explained
That I was miles away
But I'm a twerp
A fishy burp
It gave the game away

HEY TIDDLE TIDDLE

Sing to: Hey Diddle Diddle

Hey tiddle tiddle, it's time for a piddle
The silly dog laughs like a loon
He says he'll go later when his need is greater
And forgets that he's locked up till noon

❄ ❄ ❄

ONE TWO HOW I LOVE FOOD

Sing to: One Two Buckle My Shoe

One two
How I love food

Three four
Mouse in the jaw

Five six
Feel a bit sick

Seven eight
Something I ate

Nine ten
Chicken again

Eleven twelve
Meat on the shelf

Thirteen fourteen
Cream 'n' sardine

Fifteen sixteen
Licking ice cream

Seventeen eighteen
Tum vacating

Nineteen twenty
Stomach's empty!

❄ ❄ ❄

PING PONG SMELL

Sing to: Ding Dong Bell

Ping pong smell
Better wash me well

Once I'm clean
Tell you where I've been

Can't complain
Been sitting in a drain

Out of luck
Been walking in the muck

Need more spit
Been rolling in the s***

Ping pong smell
Better wash me well

❄ ❄ ❄

LET US SNACK HARDER

Sing to: Little Jack Horner

Let us snack harder
Steal from the larder
Eat all the food we deserve
We'll eat the fish paste
And gobble in haste
We only have time for hors d'oeuvres!

✳ ✳ ✳

COME! COME! IT'S HYPER FUN

Sing to: Tom Tom The Piper's Son

Come! Come! It's hyper fun
Find a tree and up we'll run
And if we make a hue and cry
They dare not leave us high and dry

Fire! Fire! The clanging bell
'Ladders up!' the firemen yell
Now up they climb to rescue us
Such fun to cause a merry fuss

Now! Now! The time is right
We pretend to get a fright
He reaches out, we run away
This is the highlight of our day

❄ ❄ ❄

THERE WAS A BIT OF FUR

Sing to: There Was a Little Girl

There was a bit of fur
And I thought I just might hurl
Right on the middle of your bedspread
But then I changed my mind
And decided to be kind
So I went to use your loo instead

❄ ❄ ❄

MY FLUFFY ABDOMEN IS RATHER TABOO

Sing to: There Was an Old Woman
Who Lived in a Shoe

My fluffy abdomen is rather taboo
Some say it's quite tubby and under review
I squeeze through my cat flap from front to the back
Then go and fill up with a nice little snack

Now I have a cousin who lives at the zoo
He's portly and really has nothing to do
I would be quite happy to end up like him
It's only a wuss who'd be wiry and slim

So eat and be merry, I do it for you
I'll double my munching of sparrow and shrew
For what would you cuddle if I did weigh less
A well-rounded moggy so full of largesse

JOLLY IF WE SETTLE ON

Sing to: Polly Put the Kettle On

Jolly if we settle on
Mummy's bed while she is gone
Clean white sheets to walk upon
With dirty feet

Someone's coming panic reigns!
In our baskets jump again
Innocence we must now feign
We've all been asleep

❄ ❄ ❄

I WORRY I HURRY A LOT

Sing to: Hickory Dickory Dock

I worry I hurry a lot
You feed me on the dot!
It's well past eight
No food on the plate
I fear that you may have forgot

❄ ❄ ❄

THE AUTHORS

Julie Hope was born in Sheffield, Yorkshire in 1952. She qualified as a furniture designer and spent many years in this profession. This not being an occupation with a high content of fun and flippancy, Julie found a convenient outlet in illustrating, cartooning, and writing whimsical verse. Her cartoons, birthday cards and Christmas cards were always of enormous delight to family, friends and colleagues. In 1982 Julie emigrated to South Africa where she later met and married John Hope, an electronics engineer. One night in 1995 the two of them wrote the songs for Christmas Carols for Cats in the back of a small notebook and on bits of paper serviette whilst dining in a Chinese restaurant in Johannesburg.

Christmas Carols for Cats was published by Bantam in 1996, but to Julie's disappointment the publisher insisted on using their in-house illustrator. Subsequent books, Nursery Rhymes for Cats, and Christmas Crackers for Cats followed the same format. In 1997 Julie and John and their four cats relocated to Oxfordshire, UK.

In 2007 John wrote his first full length book, Nine Lives, handsomely illustrated by Julie, which they self-published in September 2010. Sadly, Julie died later the same month and it was John's intention to keep Julie's work alive by continuing to write books and online media for whimsical cat lovers, using her large archive of unpublished illustrations.

John F. Hope was born in Johannesburg, South Africa in 1958 and began writing anthropomorphic stories about animals at age six, encouraged by his grade school teacher. Some of this was frowned upon by the headmaster because said stories failed the test of political correctness, even in 1964. John's other passion in life was electronics, which he enthusiastically embraced at age eight and cemented over the next few decades by becoming an electronics engineer of some skill.

In 1990 he met and married Julie, and the whimsical synergy that resulted from this union led to the publishing of three books by Bantam, Christmas Carols for Cats, Nursery Rhymes for Cats, and Christmas Crackers for Cats.

John passed away suddenly in September 2016, six years after his late wife, Julie - to the day.

Andrea Hope was born in Baildon, Yorkshire, and studied graphic design. She enjoyed a long career in this field, working in advertising, TV and package design before switching to a career in travel in the nineties. John and Andrea met and married in 2011 and another creative union developed with Andrea producing the covers for her husband's books. They lived together with their cats in Longhope, Gloucestershire until John's untimely death.

Andrea has subsequently maintained the cato9tales website, regularly posting John's astute observations, whimsical cat stories and a secret language of cats: Cat Speak. You can read these wonderful stories here: **www.cato9tales.com**

Andrea has since returned to working full time in photography, and art, producing hand drawn pastel pencil portraits of pets, babies and children.

See Andrea's work here: **www-pi-artstudios.com**

OTHER BOOKS BY THE AUTHORS
Christmas Carols for Cats
Christmas Crackers for Cats
Nine Lives
Hatching Discordia

Printed in Great Britain
by Amazon